THE LARAMIE PROJECT: TEN YEARS LATER

BY **MOISÉS KAUFMAN,**
LEIGH FONDAKOWSKI,
GREG PIEROTTI,
ANDY PARIS,
AND **STEPHEN BELBER**

★ Revised Edition

★

DRAMATISTS
PLAY SERVICE
INC.

THE LARAMIE PROJECT: TEN YEARS LATER
Copyright © 2012, 2017, Moisés Kaufman, Leigh Fondakowski,
Greg Pierotti, Andy Paris, Stephen Belber

All Rights Reserved

SPECIAL NOTE

2

Dedicated to the memory of Joseph P. Sullivan

THE FACTS

On October 6, 1998, a gay University of Wyoming student, Matthew Shepard, left the Fireside Bar with Aaron McKinney and Russell Henderson. The following day he was discovered at the edge of town. He was tied to a fence, brutally beaten, and close to death.

By the following day, Matthew's attack and the town of Laramie had become the focus of an international news story. On October 12, 1998, Matthew Shepard died at Poudre Valley Hospital in Fort Collins, Colorado.

ACKNOWLEDGMENTS

The members of Tectonic Theater Project and Moisés Kaufman thank the following people for their contributions to *The Laramie Project*:

Michael Emerson, Sarah Lambert, Maude Mitchell, Molly Powell, James Asher, Dave McKennan, Ledlie Hoffstedler, and Jan Leslie Harding for their participation at different stages of the play's development.

In Laramie, the staff of the Albany County Courthouse, the faculty and staff of the University of Wyoming Theatre Department, Catherine Connolly and her family, Rob DeBree, Philip Dubois, Tiffany Edwards, Reggie and Mike Fluty and their family, Ben Fritzen, Matt Galloway, Susanna Goodin, Larry and Carolyn Hazlett, Rebecca Hilliker and Rich Nelson, Stephen Mead Johnson, Phil Labrie, Beth Loffreda, Bob McKee, Bear and Jeri McKinney, Matt Mickelson, Jeffrey Montgomery, Garrett Neergaard, Romaine Patterson, Gene Pratt, Cathy Renna, Zackie Salmon, Jessica Sanchez, Father Roger Schmit, Jedadiah Schultz, Jonas Slonaker, Rulon Stacey, Trish and Ron Steger, Zubaida Ula, Harry Woods, and all the people of Laramie, Wyoming, who so generously opened their hearts and minds to us.

Robert Redford, Philip Himberg, Ken Brecher, Robert Blacker, Beth Nathanson, Shirley Fishman, and the staff of the Sundance Theatre Lab. They flew us to their beautiful oasis in the Utah mountains and gave us an artistic environment in which to work. Large sections of this play were written there.

In New York, Jim Nicola and New York Theatre Workshop for their belief in our work and their invitation to participate in their summer retreat at Dartmouth, where even more of this play was written. Dominick Balletta and Performance Associates for their guidance and work on our behalf. Lynne Soffer and Walton Wilson for their excellence.

In Denver, Donovan Marley, Barbara Sellers, Rick Barbour, Chris Wiger, and everyone at the Denver Center Theatre Company for producing the world premiere of *The Laramie Project*. They took on a play that was very much in progress—in fact, it had no third act—and gave us a home to finish it.

For their courageous support of the development of the play, we thank Joan Shigekawa and the Rockefeller Foundation, Rob Marx and the Fan Fox and Leslie R. Samuels Foundation, the New York State Council on the Arts, the Jeanne M. Sullivan and Joseph P. Sullivan Foundation, Anne Milliken, and Leon Levy. Roy Gabay, Gayle Francis, Mara Isaacs, Hank Unger, Mike Rego, Matt Rego, John Hart, and Jeff Sharp, who had the vision and know-how to bring *The Laramie Project* to the New York stage.

Joe and Jeanne Sullivan, for their generous and unwavering support of our creative process.

Peter Cane and Joyce Ketay for their continuous support and advice; Alan Schuster for his interest and his beautiful theater; and Kevin McAnarney for getting the word out.

To the following people and institutions for their wonderful attention to the very pragmatic things that made *The Laramie Project* possible: Marta Bell, Mérida Castillejo, Randall Kent Cohn, Gino Dilonio, Jonathan Ferrantelli, Michael Honda, Christy Meyer, Megan Spooner, Anne Stott, Courtney Watson, the Atlantic Theater Company, Access Theater, and the Church of St. Paul and St. Andrew.

AUTHORS' NOTE

The Laramie Project had its world premiere at Denver Center Theatre Company in Denver, Colorado, in 2000. At that time, none of us could have imagined the groundswell of interest and productions that would spring up from there. *The Laramie Project* has gone on to be one of the most produced plays in the country for over a decade. As writers we have often been asked—and asked ourselves—why is this so?

One answer is that interest in *The Laramie Project* is a testament to the legacy of Matthew Shepard. His life and his death brought meaning to many lives beyond Laramie.

A second answer comes directly from the participants in the productions themselves. These productions run the spectrum— from professional companies to amateur companies and community theaters to college and high school productions. In the age of social networking and the internet we often hear directly from these students—their passion for this work is remarkable. We recognize that students, teachers, and administrators have in some cases endeavored to produce *Laramie* at great personal and professional risk; the subjects of hate crime and homophobia have outlined deep divides within some communities.

Laramie is the story of an American town, but it is also the story of ordinary Americans who created a conversation unlike any that had happened up to that point in history. These were ordinary people who faced extraordinary circumstances. Matthew Shepard's murder was a moment in history that revealed both the best and worst in human character and experience.

As a theater company, we had the great privilege of speaking at length with the residents of Laramie, Wyoming, multiple times over the period of a year and a half in the aftermath of the brutal hate crime of Matthew Shepard. Those interviews provided the foundation for the writing of *The Laramie Project*.

Laramie resident Jonas Slonaker asks at the end of *The Laramie Project*: "What's come out of it? What's come out of this that's concrete or lasting?" Ten years later, we decided to return to Laramie to see how the people of the town had changed. We caught up with many of our original interviewees to talk with them again about how their town had changed. We talked to new people as well, including the perpetrators Aaron McKinney and Russell Henderson, as well as Matthew's mother, Judy Shepard.

With the tenth anniversary of Matthew Shepard's murder approaching, Moisés Kaufman, Artistic Director of Tectonic Theater Project, asked, "How does a community write its own history?" Under a microscope for ten years, having been associated with such a brutal crime, how has Laramie responded? We have heard people all over the country and all over the world say that Laramie is just like their town. How have we as a nation and as a global community responded?

The Laramie Project: Ten Years Later was written as a stand-alone play. That is, it does not have to be performed in conjunction with the original play. However, we hope that the towns and cities and schools across the country who have performed *The Laramie Project* will also perform this epilogue in their communities. And we are excited by the possibility that the two plays could run in repertory to give the full breadth and scope of Laramie's journey.

The world premiere of *The Laramie Project: Ten Years Later* took place on the eleventh anniversary of the death of Matthew Shepard. It was performed at Lincoln Center's Alice Tully Hall by the original cast of *The Laramie Project*. The play was performed simultaneously in more than one hundred and fifty theaters across the country and around the world.

We are honored to be part of this ongoing story of an American town. And we are thrilled to share this conversation with all of you.

On October 12, 2009, Tectonic Theater Project premiered THE LARAMIE PROJECT: TEN YEARS LATER simultaneously in one hundred and fifty theaters in all fifty states and eight countries. Presented by each theater with their own casts, the audience was linked with the original cast's performance at Lincoln Center's Alice Tully Hall via live streaming. In this historic theatrical nod to the Federal Theatre Project, the play was seen by fifty thousand people in one night.

At Alice Tully Hall, the performance was directed by Moisés Kaufman; the scenic consultant was Derek McClane; the lighting design was by Jason Lyons; the dramaturg was Jimmy Maize; and the producers were Greg Reiner and Tiffany Redmon. The cast was as follows:

Kelli Simpkins .... Leigh Fondakowski/Zackie Salmon/
Jan Lundhurst/Romaine Patterson/Clerk

Amanda Gronich .... Beth Loffreda/Marge Murray/
Girl/*20/20* Narrator

Greg Pierotti .... Himself/Jonas Slonaker/Rob DeBree/
University Official/Aaron McKinney*

Stephen Belber .... Himself/Cowboy/Dave O'Malley/
Friend #1/George/Republican Man

Andy Paris .... Himself/Matt Mickelson/Jedadiah Shultz/
Jim Osborne/Jerry Parkinson/Gene Pratt/
Boy/Jim/Russell Henderson/Peterson

Barbara Pitts-McAdams .... Catherine Connolly/Grandma/
Lucy Thompson/Friend #2/Ben/Judy Shepard

Mercedes Herrero .... Rebecca Hilliker/Reggie Fluty/
Deb Thomsen/Susan Swapp/Desk Mate

John McAdams .... Moisés Kaufman/Jeffrey Lockwood/
Rental Car Agent/Governor Freudenthal/
Dennis Shepard/Father Roger/Glenn Silber/
John Dorst/Childers

---

* In ensuing productions, the role of Aaron McKinney should not be part of the Greg Pierotti track but part of the Andy Paris track.

CHARACTERS

NARRATOR—played by various company members as needed.

GREG PIEROTTI—Member, Tectonic Theater Project; early forties.

BETH LOFFREDA—Professor, University of Wyoming; author of the book *Losing Matt Shepard*; early forties.

MOISÉS KAUFMAN—Artistic Director, Tectonic Theater Project; early forties.

STEPHEN BELBER—Member, Tectonic Theater Project; early forties.

LEIGH FONDAKOWSKI—Member, Tectonic Theater Project; late thirties.

MATT MICKELSON—Former owner of the Fireside Bar; forties.

MARGE MURRAY—Mother of police officer Reggie Fluty; late sixties.

JEFFREY LOCKWOOD—Laramie resident; fifties.

JEDADIAH SHULTZ—Laramie native; University of Wyoming theater student now living in NYC; early thirties.

REBECCA HILLIKER—Theater professor, University of Wyoming; fifties.

ZACKIE SALMON—Laramie resident, originally from Texas; advocate for domestic partner benefits on campus; fifties.

ANDY PARIS—Member, Tectonic Theater Project; late thirties.

COWBOY—Laconic man on the street; late forties.

RENTAL CAR AGENT—Retired military; early seventies.

REGGIE FLUTY—Police officer who found Matthew Shepard at the fence; retired; late forties.

JONAS SLONAKER—Openly gay Laramie resident; late forties.

DEB THOMSEN—Editor of the *Laramie Boomerang*, local Laramie newspaper; early fifties.

GOVERNOR FREUDENTHAL—Governor of Wyoming; fifties.

DAVE O'MALLEY—Retired Laramie police officer, lead investigator on the Matthew Shepard case for Laramie Police Department; early fifties.

CATHERINE CONNOLLY—Out lesbian professor, University of Wyoming; member of the Wyoming Legislature; fifties.

ROB DEBREE—Lead investigator on the Matthew Shepard case for the Albany County Sheriff's Department; early fifties.

JIM OSBORNE—Friend of Matthew Shepard; Laramie resident; mid-thirties.

FRIEND #1—Friend of Jim Osborne; early thirties.

GRANDMA—Grandmother of Friend #1; late seventies.

MOM—A Laramie housewife; early forties.

DENNIS SHEPARD—Father of Matthew Shepard; fifties.

JERRY PARKINSON—Dean of the law school, University of Wyoming; advocate for domestic partner benefits; late forties.

UNIVERSITY OFFICIAL—Late fifties.

FATHER ROGER—Catholic priest at the Catholic Newman Center in Laramie at the time of Matthew Shepard's murder; sixties.

LUCY THOMPSON—Grandmother of convicted murderer, Russell Henderson; seventies.

BOY—Current student at University of Wyoming; late teens.

GIRL—Current student at University of Wyoming; late teens.

STUDENT—Another student at the University of Wyoming.

JAN LUNDHURST—Laramie resident; late forties.

20/20 NARRATOR—Newscaster; late thirties.

GLENN SILBER—Producer, *20/20*; early fifties.

ROMAINE PATTERSON—Friend of Matthew Shepard; gay activist; early thirties.

BOOMERANG EDITOR—Played by actor who plays Deb Thomsen; early fifties.

FRIEND #2—Friend of Jim Osborne; early twenties.

JOHN DORST—Professor, University of Wyoming; folklorist and Laramie resident; mid-fifties.

GEORGE—Laramie resident; guest at potluck dinner party; fifties.

BEN—Laramie resident; guest at potluck dinner party; forties.

JIM—Laramie resident; guest at potluck dinner party; forties.

SUSAN SWAPP—University of Wyoming professor and Laramie resident; mid-fifties.

NIKKI ELDER—Teacher, Laramie High School; early thirties.

RUSSELL HENDERSON—Convicted murderer of Matthew Shepard; early thirties.

CLERK—Chief clerk in Wyoming Legislature; mid-thirties.

PETERSON—Republican representative in Wyoming Legislature; late sixties.

DESK MATE—Catherine Connolly's desk mate in the Legislature; early forties.

CONSERVATIVE COLLEAGUE—Catherine Connolly's colleague in the Legislature; early fifties.

CHILDERS—Conservative representative in Wyoming Legislature; early seventies.

REPUBLICAN MAN—Catherine Connolly's colleague in Wyoming Legislature; early fifties.

OTHER REPRESENTATIVES OF WYOMING LEGISLATURE—Voting on Resolution 17.

AARON MCKINNEY—Convicted murderer of Matthew Shepard; early thirties.

JUDY SHEPARD—Mother of Matthew Shepard; fifties.

THE LARAMIE PROJECT: TEN YEARS LATER

ACT ONE

The sound of wind. The sound of many voices speaking. At first in whispers, then a little louder. Lights come up onstage. The space is littered with chairs. All facing the audience. They suggest the homes and the characters that inhabit Laramie. Beth Loffreda enters. She's wearing a coat or a vest to protect her from the cold. She looks around, remembering.

Moment: The Light This Fall

BETH LOFFREDA. I am thinking about the anniversary a lot. Ten years have passed...that's a long time. *(Pause.)* The light this fall is much like the light that fall and we've been having days that remind me of that fall when Matt was killed...so there's something about the elemental reality here that feels intensely like that September and October when all of this happened. That was 1998. *(Pause. Pointing out her window.)* You can see the prairie and the foothills from some offices on campus. You can look out the window and you can see a little patch of the foothills, you know, past Walmart, where Matthew died.

So what happened here still feels very present to me.

My gut reaction is that Laramie is a somewhat better place to be than it was ten years ago, but I don't know how to tell the story of the past ten years without having to think about, both what we've done, but also what we haven't done. *(Transition. The company enters.)*

Moment: Good Energy

MOISÉS KAUFMAN. September twelfth. On our way to Laramie again.

NARRATOR. Company member Moisés Kaufman.

MOISÉS KAUFMAN. The anniversary of Matthew's death is exactly one month away. Arriving into town off Highway 80, I am surprised by how much the town has grown.

LEIGH FONDAKOWSKI. There is an explosion of new development on the east side.

NARRATOR. Company member Leigh Fondakowski.

LEIGH FONDAKOWSKI. At least three brand-new hotels and several strip malls. Walmart has been replaced by Super Walmart.

MATT MICKELSON. How has Laramie changed?

NARRATOR. Matt Mickelson, former owner of the Fireside Bar.

MATT MICKELSON. These days in Wyoming with the coal-bed methane boom and—the energy industry—like Dick Cheney sold half our state to Halliburton. But people don't seem to mind.

MARGE MURRAY. Yeah, they're drillin' all over now.

NARRATOR. Marge Murray.

MARGE MURRAY. They are and they should. And we have so much coal that it's unreal. No matter where you go, you poke a hole in the ground and you'll find some coal. And it's good energy.

JEFFREY LOCKWOOD. The position Wyoming is in right now economically, there's plenty of money.

NARRATOR. Laramie resident Jeffrey Lockwood.

JEFFREY LOCKWOOD. The recession hasn't touched us here. We've been having a big energy boom and they're talking about it being a thirty-year boom.

JEDEDIAH SCHULTZ. The entire shape of Laramie has changed.

NARRATOR. Laramie native Jedadiah Schultz.

JEDEDIAH SCHULTZ. We have a Chili's now. Laramie has a lot more of those kinds of—like little modern mini-mall things. The university is booming with money so they just build, build, build and they've got a huge Hilton and a Holiday Inn and a convention center.

JEFFREY LOCKWOOD. Now, some of these communities that

they're drilling in are just getting hammered in terms of the environment—the goose that's laying the golden egg is crapping all over you but it's still producing golden eggs.

REBECCA HILLIKER. On the surface things have changed here.

NARRATOR. Rebecca Hilliker, theater department, University of Wyoming.

REBECCA HILLIKER. Just look around you at the physical growth. But whether or not we have changed the underlying culture of Wyoming at all, I don't know.

JIM OSBORNE. After the media storm died down here in Laramie—

NARRATOR. Jim Osborne, friend of Matthew Shepard.

JIM OSBORNE. There were a lot of folks who simply didn't want to talk about Matthew Shepard anymore. They were tired of their community and their lives being the nightly news. They were tired of feeling the stigma of having such a heinous crime occur in our community.

JOHN DORST. This was all anyone talked about in terms of what Laramie is and Wyoming is.

NARRATOR. Laramie resident John Dorst.

JOHN DORST. There was I think a palpable sense here in Laramie of just, "Let's stop talking about this, please, let's return to business as usual."

Moment: Reggie and Marge

NARRATOR. Company member Greg Pierotti.

GREG PIEROTTI. I drive out to meet with Reggie Fluty, the officer who found Matthew Shepard at the fence.

REGGIE FLUTY. Well, I am no longer working on the force now.

GREG PIEROTTI. Really?

REGGIE FLUTY. Yep. I'm retired.

MARGE MURRAY. Her horses are her work now.

GREG PIEROTTI. We also speak with her mom, Marge Murray.

MARGE MURRAY. Ask her what she named her horses—

GREG PIEROTTI. What'd you name your horses?

REGGIE FLUTY. Boogeyman, Reno, and Mad Marge.

MARGE MURRAY. She named a horse after me.

REGGIE FLUTY. I told her, "I am riding a horse that reminds me of you on a bad day."

MARGE MURRAY. *(Smiling.)* The brat... And she still has her llamas—

REGGIE FLUTY. And we have a couple of new colts.

MARGE MURRAY. But you asked us how our lives have changed? Biggest change would be Reggie's not working on the force now.

REGGIE FLUTY. After I retired, I had to learn how to sleep again and how to be a normal citizen again. Not live in code yellow like everywhere you go somebody's ready to sucker punch you, you know?

MARGE MURRAY. After Shepard, it was hell for her. And after the main crisis was over, every time there was a high-profile case, like girls getting raped or babies dying—they only knew one phone number: Reggie's. So it finally got to her.

REGGIE FLUTY. I did those kinds of cases for so long that I got exhausted. Those can burn you out pretty fast. Now the horses, they don't give a damn if I am a police officer or an ordinary citizen. You know, with them, it's all about "When's feedin' time?"

But as far as Laramie is concerned, I do think people's views have changed. I think we were so embarrassed the first time that we don't want that to happen again. And sometimes you know, you gotta just as a community get the snot slugged out of you before you wake up and grow up, you know?

MARGE MURRAY. Well, there were two things, though, that I really hated. Tearing that fence down and not puttin' up some kind of...something to say "This is where it happened. Straighten up, Laramie."

GREG PIEROTTI. They took the fence down?

MARGE MURRAY. Yeah, they did.

REGGIE FLUTY. The owner didn't want people coming out onto his property to see it—there's "no trespassing" signs all over there now.

GREG PIEROTTI. Wow.

REGGIE FLUTY. I just hope the community remembers truly how ugly hate is. Every time there's an anniversary of his death, talk comes back up. And it makes people have to own what they think. If you hang around Laramie long enough, you'll know where everybody stands.

Moment: Second and Garfield (Cowboy)

NARRATOR. Company member Andy Paris.

ANDY PARIS. One of the first things we do when we get to Laramie this time is walk around the town conducting informal interviews. Moisés and I are waiting out a storm under the awning of the Laramie Health Clinic on Second and Garfield. A cowboy steps out of the clinic for a smoke.

ANDY PARIS. Good afternoon.

COWBOY. How ya doin'.

ANDY PARIS. Just waitin' out the rain under here.

MOISÉS KAUFMAN. We're here from New York with a theater company. *(Pause. Cowboy doesn't answer.)* We're here finding out how Laramie has changed since the Matthew Shepard murder. *(Pause. Cowboy doesn't answer.)* Can we ask you a couple of questions? *(Pause.)*

COWBOY. No. *(Cowboy goes back inside.)*

ANDY PARIS. That went well.

Moment: Third and Custer

RENTAL CAR AGENT. Mid-sized car okay for you, Mr. Belber?

STEPHEN BELBER. That'll be just fine.

RENTAL CAR AGENT. You're here for the big game?

STEPHEN BELBER. Actually, I'm here with a theater company, we are writing a play about the town ten years after the death of Matthew Shepard.

RENTAL CAR AGENT. Well, I wish you luck with your project, but I do think it's time to let the boy go. Now if you ask me, I think it was robbery and that his lifestyle was just an excuse. His lifestyle's beside the point. It makes no difference to me.

STEPHEN BELBER. Do you think it made a difference to his killers?

RENTAL CAR AGENT. No, I don't. No. I think they set out to

rob him, found out about his lifestyle, and then in the trial used it as an excuse…

STEPHEN BELBER. *(Surprised.)* I'm not sure I understand. Are you saying that it wasn't a hate crime?

RENTAL CAR AGENT. Well, I just think people have agendas and they keep coming here pushing their agendas and they're keeping that boy stuck. I think it's time to let the boy go. I think it's time to let go and let the young man get on with his life—or with his death—'course, I believe in an afterlife.

Excuse me but I have to attend to this gentleman. You enjoy your stay in Laramie.

STEPHEN BELBER. Thank you.

Moment: *Boomerang* #1—Deb Thomsen

MOISÉS KAUFMAN. With the anniversary of Matthew's death approaching, I call Deb Thomsen, the editor of the main paper here in Laramie.

DEB THOMSEN. *Laramie Boomerang.*

MOISÉS KAUFMAN. Hi, may I please speak with Deb?

DEB THOMSEN. Speaking.

MOISÉS KAUFMAN. Deb, this is Moisés Kaufman, how are you?

DEB THOMSEN. *(Pause. Hesitates.)* Hi, I'm fine, thanks.

MOISÉS KAUFMAN. Good. So do you have a moment to talk?

DEB THOMSEN. No problem.

MOISÉS KAUFMAN. So tell me, as editor of the main paper here in Laramie, how have the people been thinking about the anniversary?

DEB THOMSEN. Actually, we're doing a short series. I'm doing the intro piece and one of the other reporters has been talking with people just to get their perspective now.

MOISÉS KAUFMAN. And besides the series, what kinds of events are planned for the anniversary of Matthew's murder?

DEB THOMSEN. Well…events…here in Laramie? That would be more something that is organized on campus. But to be quite honest with you, we're long past this… You know, we're trying to put this behind us, and keep going. You have brutality and you deal with it, and you move on.

19

MOISÉS KAUFMAN. Mm hmm?

DEB THOMSEN. I do think that it brought forth a different awareness... I hesitate to speak on behalf of the community, but I don't believe that the catalyst was homosexuality.

MOISÉS KAUFMAN. What do you mean?

DEB THOMSEN. I really believe they wanted money. And Matthew didn't have what they thought and it just escalated to an anger that was totally out of control. There was so much speculation about drug use. I just don't think it was about his sexuality.

MOISÉS KAUFMAN. *(Surprised.)* So you don't think it was a hate crime?

DEB THOMSEN. I think everything is a hate crime. You have to have some kind of hatred in you to do that to another human being. As far as where that hatred comes from, I really couldn't tell you. Most people in the community, they're aware of what's happened here, they know that the anniversary is coming up, but we really are moving on from this.

Moment: Measuring Change #1

NARRATOR. Leigh Fondakowski.

LEIGH FONDAKOWSKI. I drive up to Cheyenne, the state capitol, to speak with Wyoming Governor Dave Freudenthal.

(To governor.) Governor, one of the things we are hearing in Laramie is some people now saying that this was not a hate crime.

GOVERNOR FREUDENTHAL. I haven't heard that. *(Beat.)* I don't know where you are hearing that. It may be that there are people who want to dismiss it. I don't share that view. It happened here. And we have to own that. When people think about Matthew Shepard's murder, it's not a particularly proud moment in the state's history or the community's history.

And I would say that there has been a change in general in the state with regard to more thoughtful discussion. If you just say the words "Matthew Shepard" it registers with people. At least people in my generation. I can tell you that it has a different feel about how we talk about things.

How do you *measure* change is the thing I'm stuck with.

I mean, the events surrounding the death of Matthew Shepard changed us—it clearly did. How you measure that change, I'm not quite sure.

DAVE O' MALLEY. *(Answering the governor, enthusiastically.)* Well, I tell you what, we now have the AIDS Walk here in Laramie, it's in its sixth year, okay?

NARRATOR. Dave O'Malley, retired Laramie police officer.

DAVE O' MALLEY. And it's grown. Last year we raised around twenty-two thousand dollars. And five thousand dollars at drag queen bingo alone! I mean we had the drag queens at the Cowboy Bar, Jim and Jason and Travis, and they put on just a great production you know. Yeah, at the *Cowboy* Bar!

CATHERINE CONNOLLY. On campus the biggest difference would be the symposium for social justice.

NARRATOR. Catherine Connolly, university professor.

CATHERINE CONNOLLY. The name changed to the *Shepard* Symposium on Social Justice several years ago, and not only is it a university conference but kids from all over Wyoming are coming to the Shepard Symposium. Great big yellow school buses of kids coming in to hear these speakers talk about justice and social change. And you get thousands of people from the town participating, and for this town, that's a lot of people. So, I'm giving you the good.

JIM OSBORNE. Before Matt's murder, nobody talked much about gay and lesbian people or issues in Wyoming.

NARRATOR. Jim Osborne, friend of Matthew Shepard.

JIM OSBORNE. Now, there's a Rainbow Resource Center on campus, we have more gender and sexuality classes, the high school has a gay-straight alliance. I am openly gay. And I've heard from a lot of folks in Laramie over the years who say to me things like:

FRIEND #1. Jim, my grandmother watched a news story and she called me and she said:

GRANDMA. You know what, honey, I just wanted you to know it doesn't matter to me if you're gay.

FRIEND #1. But Grandma, I'm straight.

GRANDMA. Well, but if you were.

FRIEND #1. Well, thank you Grandma.

JIM OSBORNE. Or folks who come to me and say:

MOM. My husband makes...comments. What if my five-year-old son happens to grow up to be gay? I don't want him to be afraid his father's going to hate him. How can I let my kids know that it's okay with me, you know?

JIM OSBORNE. So we don't have a hate crimes law on the books, but the conversations that go on in our locker rooms, in the hallways at schools, on the playgrounds, in our living rooms, and places of worship. That to me is progress.

Moment: Safe Pocket

JONAS SLONAKER. For me the biggest change from then to now is that I am completely out now.

NARRATOR. Jonas Slonaker.

JONAS SLONAKER. After Matt was killed I was gonna leave Laramie. But I went to the vigil for Matthew Shepard and I met Bill there... *(Smile.)* We started seeing each other...and we have been together ever since—ten years. Everybody knows that Bill is my boyfriend, but I am in a safe pocket and the safe pocket is the university. I'm in student affairs and that's a really safe place to be. Now if I were in Ag? Agriculture? It would be different. Or you know if I worked at the cement factory here in Laramie, it's a different world. But I mean, finding your safe pockets is what we do as gay people, not just here in Laramie, but wherever we live.

Moment: Bench Dedication

ANDY PARIS. With the anniversary of Matthew's death now only two weeks away, we spoke to Beth Loffreda about what the university is doing to mark the day.

BETH LOFFREDA. The university held a ceremony dedicating a memorial bench in the name of Matthew Shepard. The bench is tucked away in a remote corner of the campus. It was a small ceremony. There were only about fifty people there. It was a Saturday morning. It was chilly and then, in that way that happens here in Laramie as if a switch has been flipped, all at once blazingly warm.

There was a podium beside the bench. Dennis Shepard spoke. When he got up to speak, you could see that his nose was scratched and bruised.

DENNIS SHEPARD. *(Soberly.)* Good morning. Judy and I both attended University of Wyoming and we loved it. It's nice to be back on campus again. As you can see, I had a little accident. I broke my nose doing work around the house. My son Matt and I had a competition when he was alive. We each had broken our noses twice; one of us would pull ahead of the other for a while and then the other would tie it back up again. And Matt would make fun of me for being behind. *(Pause.)* When Matt was lying in the hospital, unconscious, one of his many injuries was a broken nose. It was Matt's third, one more than me. Now I have restored the tie. *(Beat.)* This is a place for people to come. If they are aware of who Matt was. This is a place where they can come and sit and think. A lot of people come to Laramie and they want go out and find the fence. Well, the fence is no longer there. So what they can do instead is they can come here. *(Beat.)* Matt was just a normal—a normal kid who had dreams and ambitions. He wanted to work overseas—to promote the country that he loved. He wasn't ashamed of who he was. Or, who he loved. *(Beat.)* We want to thank you all for attending this morning. We hope people enjoy the bench.

ZACKIE SALMON. Matthew's legacy—his main legacy is right here at the University of Wyoming.

NARRATOR. Zackie Salmon.

ZACKIE SALMON. And I just felt there was a certain forgetfulness in the air that morning the bench was dedicated…because we've worked, worked, worked, worked, worked to get domestic partner benefits here on campus, and we still don't have that.

BETH LOFFREDA. If there was gonna be a place that I would have expected change to happen more quickly…it would be right here at the University of Wyoming.

ZACKIE SALMON. Those of us who have been fighting for this, we call ourselves the "gang of four"—and that's Beth Loffreda, myself, Cathy Connolly, and Jerry Parkinson, dean of the law school.

JERRY PARKINSON. We were all optimistic after last year with the Domestic Partner Initiative. We brought in a consultant to tell us how to get domestic partner benefits and we came up with a plan.

CATHERINE CONNOLLY. And at the start of the semester, we thought we were gonna have this implemented.

JERRY PARKINSON. But just when it's about to come to a vote, they tell us:

UNIVERSITY OFFICIAL. There's gonna be a couple of trustees who are totally opposed to this on moral grounds, and we don't agree with their views but…give us some time to talk to those folks and talk about the business necessity.

JERRY PARKINSON. *(To university official.)* Look, sooner or later you just have to take a vote and the two or three trustees who are gonna vote against it are gonna show their true colors.

UNIVERSITY OFFICIAL. Okay. We don't want them saying things about domestic partner benefits in the press that could hurt the cause. We don't know what they'll do.

JERRY PARKINSON. *(To university official.)* They're the ones who look bad in this deal. It's not the people proposing the domestic partner benefits that look bad.

ZACKIE SALMON. What about people like me? I have been with my partner Anne for twenty years and she doesn't get any of my benefits. You don't seem too worried about upsetting me?

UNIVERSITY OFFICIAL. We have all the sympathy in the world, Zackie, and we understand, but look, we don't want to run the risk if we push this too precipitously.

ZACKIE SALMON. It's been ten years that we've been fighting. This is not the 1950s anymore. It's time for Laramie to come into the twenty-first century. A bench to Matthew Shepard is nice—but a university's values are reflected in its policies.

JERRY PARKINSON. There are so many people out there around the country who don't know anything about Laramie. But they really believe in their hearts that the University of Wyoming would be the last place in the country to adopt same-sex partner benefits. And at the rate we're goin'…we *are* gonna be the last.

BETH LOFFREDA. A lot of us who work here at the university and a lot of administrators can look out our windows and can see the place where Matthew Shepard died, where he was slaughtered; I just think if that's not enough to get you off the blocks to *really* make some active significant changes on your campus…I don't know what it takes.

DENNIS SHEPARD. There is a plaque here which reads, "Matthew Wayne Shepard, December first, 1976, to October twelfth, 1998. Beloved son, brother, and friend. He continues to make a difference. Peace be with him and all who sit here." Thank you very much.

Moment: Next Generation

Acting note: These students should not be played dumb or for laughs. They should be played as regular college kids who have not been given information about this one issue.

NARRATOR. Greg Pierotti.

GREG PIEROTTI. I walk around campus to see if I can meet some students—to talk with the next generation about how they see things now...

I see a young couple getting into their car. Excuse me, can I ask you: Did you happen to attend the bench dedication for Matthew Shepard?

BOY. Excuse me.

GIRL. For who?

GREG PIEROTTI. For Matthew Shepard. *(Pause.)* Do you remember him or what happened to him?

BOY. I don't know anything about him.

GREG PIEROTTI. You never heard anything?

BOY. I heard the name, that's about it.

GREG PIEROTTI. How about you?

GIRL. I heard he was homosexual and he got murdered. He got put somewhere like on a post somewhere *(She points vaguely toward the campus.)* and he got murdered.

GREG PIEROTTI. And how long have you been at the university?

GIRL. Two years.

GREG PIEROTTI. How about you?

BOY. Yeah, two years. *(Another student walks by.)*

GREG PIEROTTI. I talked to a number of other students about what they remembered:

STUDENT. One thing I heard was that he was a drug dealer and did some bad deals and those guys ended up coming after him.

GREG PIEROTTI. So you don't think this murder was about Matthew being gay?

STUDENT. I'm not saying that's right. I am just telling you what I heard.

GREG PIEROTTI. Okay.

STUDENT. And then the media came in and said it was 'cause he was gay for their own ends. They took this as a vehicle.

GREG PIEROTTI. And you heard this from?

STUDENT. It seems like there are a lot of students sayin' it so I figured they knew what they were talking about.

Moment: *20/20*

NARRATOR. Cathy Connolly.

CATHERINE CONNOLLY. There was a generation or two generations of students who came to this university believing that the story of Matthew Shepard was relevant. That this was part of their history and they wanted to know more about it. And they were aware that they were in the same rooms, walking the same little paths that both Matthew and the perpetrators walked. But now, new students don't come to the university either knowing or caring or thinking it's relevant to their lives...

Because here is what else is going on with Matthew Shepard.

There was a *20/20* episode that came out in 2004—six years after Matthew was killed—and the implication of that TV program was that it wasn't a hate crime, but a robbery or drug deal gone bad. And people here in Laramie at that time were pretty livid given the inaccuracies.

DAVE O' MALLEY. When *20/20* called me for an interview...

NARRATOR. Dave O'Malley, lead investigator on the Shepard case for the Laramie Police Department.

DAVE O' MALLEY. I asked them "What exactly are you all doing?" And they said:

GLENN SILBER. It's an objective, what's-going-on-six-years-after type of a thing.

DAVE O' MALLEY. They came to our house and the producer Glenn Silber and Elizabeth Vargas and my wife, Jen, and I sat at *that* table. *(He points to his living-room table.)* And I asked them, "Is there any specific focus that you are directing this piece to?"

GLENN SILBER. No no no no, don't worry about that.

DAVE O' MALLEY. And Elizabeth Vargas went in our bathroom

and changed clothes and we set up and did the interview. And shortly into it, it popped straight to the methamphetamine thing.
20/20 NARRATOR. November twenty-sixth, 2004—Good evening and welcome to *20/20*.

The killing of Matthew Shepard was widely perceived as a hate crime, because Matthew was gay, but over the next hour, you will hear a very different account from the killers themselves and from new sources that have come forward for the first time. A *20/20* investigation uncovers stunning new information about one of this country's most infamous murders.

You may think you know what happened next, but you haven't heard the whole story.

JAN LUNDHURST. It was very shocking to me to see that.

NARRATOR. Laramie resident Jan Lundhurst.

JAN LUNDHURST. They were interviewing the murderers after they'd been in prison for many years, and I thought, well, yeah, you can change your story however you want to now. They completely changed what they had said in their confessions.

DAVE O' MALLEY. It angered me more than anything the things *20/20 didn't* say—the things they left out. I mean how do you come in and a) lie to me but b) put a piece together that's based solely on meth heads from the Buckhorn Bar and two convicted murderers. And I'm just goin' "Holy crap!" *(Holding up the email.)* After they left I found a hard copy of an email from Glenn Silber to Elizabeth Vargas, and I can give you a copy of it, it said:

GLENN SILBER. Although Dave is a highly skilled investigator and was the key to solving the crime quickly, he fell into the hate crimes motivation early and our piece will ultimately discredit that flawed theory.

DAVE O' MALLEY. And I read that and I went these assho—excuse me…I…get a little angry. These guys sit in my house…and lie to me. And Silber drives all the way back to Colorado and our phone rings and he says:

GLENN SILBER. Uhh… Did we leave anything there?

DAVE O' MALLEY. And I said, "Yeah and my wife has already scanned it and sent it to Judy Shepard, and she sent it to her attorney in D.C. and you can come back and get it if you want to." And he drove all the way back from Denver and—I-I-I'm not a violent individual but I really did want to choke him. *(Beat.)* And we used to watch *20/20* every week…

JIM OSBORNE. Some folks here in Laramie want to find any excuse as to why this happened.

NARRATOR. Jim Osborne, friend of Matthew Shepard.

JIM OSBORNE. They want to write this murder off. And a big part of how people do that is *20/20.*

You had a major, respected news source who came up with this set of stories that said, "Okay, it wasn't really about the fact that he was gay, it was really about *this.*"

DAVE O' MALLEY. PBS did a nice rebuttal, they went point by point through the entire thing pointing out the false statements, the leading questions, the quotes taken out of context...but how many people watch PBS and how many people watch *20/20*?

CATHERINE CONNOLLY. *(Frustrated.)* There were facts revealed in the trial, the reality of the actual confession, everything that happened in the trial gave us the truth...and we thought because it was the truth and the truth played out here—that the truth would prevail. But the reality is, that over time, that *20/20* piece has made a tremendous negative impact on how Matthew Shepard's murder is perceived. And this is—this is personal—there's a perception and belief now that it was a drug deal gone bad and that's all. So you asked me how I felt? I go catatonic after things like this. This is our history.

Moment: Father Roger

NARRATOR. Greg Pierotti.

GREG PIEROTTI. Today I spoke to Father Roger, the Catholic priest who hosted the vigil for Matthew in Laramie ten years ago, and who also visited with Aaron McKinney in jail, counseled him. Father Roger is no longer in Laramie. I spoke to him by phone.

FATHER ROGER. I left Laramie in 2002. I took a sabbatical and then I was placed in Kansas City.

GREG PIEROTTI. And where did you go on sabbatical?

FATHER ROGER. To Menlo Park, the Vatican II Institute. A great place. If you ever get ordained as a Catholic priest, Greg, go there for your sabbatical.

GREG PIEROTTI. *(Beat.)* Father, I just completely lost my train of thought. *(Beat.)* Oh yeah, how have you been changed personally by this?

FATHER ROGER. I'm much more courageous now than I was before Matthew. I talk about sexual identity a lot more. I don't talk about it every Sunday, but I do talk about it whenever the scriptures enable it to happen.

GREG PIEROTTI. Do you miss Laramie, Father?

FATHER ROGER. Oh my, yes, I miss Laramie. I will always miss Laramie.

GREG PIEROTTI. And are you still in touch with Aaron McKinney?

FATHER ROGER. Yes, I have visited with Aaron often, went to see him a bunch of times. Aaron was in Rawlins, Wyoming, for a couple of years, and now he is in Virginia, and we still write.

GREG PIEROTTI. Do you think we should try to interview him?

FATHER ROGER. Should you try? I hope you do. And let me tell you why. Aaron McKinney and Russell Henderson are products of our society. They are our brothers also. I don't say this in any way at all to excuse him; if you hear that, you are misunderstanding me. But to understand does not mean to agree with. To understand does not mean to be permissive. But to understand also isn't the kind of thing that you decide in your office. To understand Aaron, you have to visit him.

GREG PIEROTTI. I'll send Aaron a letter today asking if he would be willing to meet with me.

FATHER ROGER. Yes Greg, I think you *must* do that. I think you must. *(Beat.)* Let me give you an analogy. Several years ago a man came into our monastery and shot four of our monks, and then went into our church and shot himself. When the investigators came to take the bodies away, one of them asked Abbot Gregory, "Well, listen, we'll bring a separate vehicle to take the body of the person who killed them." And Gregory said, "No, he too is our brother. You can put them all in the same ambulance." Now you go back to this. Matthew is our brother; Russell is our brother; Aaron is our brother. And Greg, Aaron is much more like me than unlike me.

Moment: Lucy Thompson

STEPHEN BELBER. As Greg was talking to Father Roger, I was trying to find a way to talk to Russell Henderson. And so I met again with Gene Pratt, who was Russell Henderson's Mormon home teacher. After the murders, Russell was excommunicated from the Mormon Church. But Mr. Pratt remained close to the family. This time around he did something he hadn't been willing to do ten years earlier. He set up a meeting with Lucy Thompson, Russell's grandmother.

LEIGH FONDAKOWSKI. She was much older and frailer than the woman we'd seen read a statement at Russell's sentencing ten years earlier.

STEPHEN BELBER. On her wall there were pencil sketchings of Jesus—finely drawn, exquisitely detailed.

LUCY THOMPSON. Russell did those drawings in jail and sent them to me. Aren't they something? I tried to mail him some pencils and some sketchbooks. But he can't have art supplies where he's at now in Virginia. When he was in Rawlins he could. He got his GED in Rawlins too and he went to take college classes, chose his courses, got his books sent and was all excited, and then they said, "All right, it's time for you to be transferred." That happened to him twice. So he never did get to do that—go to college.

STEPHEN BELBER. Mrs. Thompson, we would very much like to interview Russell. Do you think he would talk to us?

LUCY THOMPSON. *(Pause.)* I don't know. You can try writing to him. And I'll tell him that we talked today, he calls me pretty regularly. But it will be up to him.

STEPHEN BELBER. Thank you.

Moment: *Boomerang* #2—"Our View"

NARRATOR. Andy Paris.

ANDY PARIS. Over the course of our stay in Laramie, there had been a couple of articles printed in the *Laramie Boomerang* about Matthew Shepard. These were the articles that the editor Deb Thomsen had mentioned to Moisés. This morning, on October twelfth, the tenth anniversary of Matthew's death, I got a call from Jonas Slonaker. And he said:

JONAS SLONAKER. Did you see the *Laramie Boomerang* this morning? You've got to read the editorial. You're not going to believe it, it's called:

BOOMERANG EDITOR. "Our View. Laramie is a community, not a 'project.'"

The recent news story in the *Boomerang* looking back to the brutal murder of Matthew Shepard ten years ago has drawn a wide range of reactions from this community. The biggest reaction has come from those who don't understand why this anniversary qualifies as news.

Some callers have requested that their paper delivery be held during the week that the series of stories was being published. Others have accepted that the local newspaper had to do a story about the anniversary given the national notoricty but wished that the coverage could have been less detailed and displayed more discreetly.

JONAS SLONAKER. Can you believe that?

BOOMERANG EDITOR. A far smaller number of messages have come from people who wanted much more exhaustive reporting.

Direct observation and discussion with the wide range of local residents tells us that Laramie is like most communities but more tolerant than most. That doesn't mean there aren't prejudiced or bigoted people here. There are. But those people don't define Laramie, and it is infuriating for those of us who consider this our home to be labeled because of the actions of a few questionable characters.

That label is particularly galling in this case because the crime in question has been portrayed in the national media as a homophobic attack and as a hate crime because Matthew Shepard was homosexual. But no one can know that motivation except for the two men who committed the crime.

JONAS SLONAKER. Andy, they had a trial and it was established as a hate crime. That's why they had a trial. That's what a trial is for, so that we can learn these things!

BOOMERANG EDITOR. Police records certainly seem to indicate that this was a robbery that went very bad.

JONAS SLONAKER. What police records are they referring to? A robbery? I tie you up and smash your head in because I want to rob you? It's absurd! And this is Laramie's main newspaper.

BOOMERANG EDITOR. But those who wanted to label Laramie as a bigoted town in the Wild West didn't let the facts get in the way of their stories. So who then is guilty of intolerance and perpetuating stereotypes?

JONAS SLONAKER. *(Angry.)* A robbery gone bad over drugs, that's denial. That's some kind of massive denial.

ANDY PARIS. Jonas wrote a letter to the editor.

JONAS SLONAKER. Many citizens of Laramie want to move on but denial isn't the best way to accomplish that. There is no disgrace for Laramie in acknowledging that part or all of the motivation in the murder of Matthew Shepard was homophobia. NO, the crime certainly does not define Laramie. How we react to the crime, how we talk about it, and if we do or don't do anything to prevent this from happening again does define Laramie.

ANDY PARIS. Then he told me:

JONAS SLONAKER. Andy, I can't wait to hear what people say when my letter goes to print.

Moment: Visible Markers

NARRATOR. Stephen Belber.

STEPHEN BELBER. I spend the afternoon with Matt Mickelson, former owner of the Fireside Bar. The fence has been taken down. The Fireside, where Matthew met his killers, has been renamed JJ's. It seems like all the visible markers of Matthew's death are gone.

MATT MICKELSON. Yeah, I had to sell the Fireside. On one side people were like, "Local Gay Bar!" and then on the other they're like, "Crazy Redneck Gay Slayers!" For seven years—I tried to ride that shit out. Then, MTV'd make a movie, so I'd renovate and paint and do all this shit. Then HBO'd make a movie. NBC'd make a movie. *20/20*'d make a movie. They drug that shit out for seven fuckin' years—so, instead of havin' kids crawlin' in the windows on a Friday night, it was a ghost town. Man, I did eight hundred and some thousand dollars in sales that year that Matt was killed. The next year I did forty-three thousand, crushed me. I had to put that shit up for sale.

STEPHEN BELBER. And then I asked Mickelson about the *Boomerang* editorial:

MATT MICKELSON. I tried to tell people—it was such a big media sensationalism hate crime hate crime hate crime—it's not—that wasn't the issue. The issue was methamphetamines. They'd been up for three days, those two guys had been up for three days doin' dope. And that's why they beat him and robbed him.

NARRATOR. Jim Osborne.

JIM OSBORNE. One of my friends a couple months back said to me:

FRIEND #2. I know what really happened, I've talked with people, I know what really happened. It was drugs.

JIM OSBORNE. And I looked at her and I said, "You were eight when Matt was killed. How in the hell do you know what really happened? You were eight and not living in this town. But somehow you know?"

REGGIE FLUTY. Yeah, I've heard about people who say it wasn't a hate crime.

NARRATOR. Reggie Fluty.

REGGIE FLUTY. Nobody says that to me. And if they do, it gets shut down so fast. I won't discuss it. It's not an option, it's bullshit and I'm not wasting my time or theirs.

Moment: *Boomerang* #3—The Story We've Told Ourselves

JONAS SLONAKER. I waited all week for the *Laramie Boomerang* to print my letter. And it finally got to the next Sunday and it never appeared. And there was a letter from a guy lamenting the fact that not enough people are coming to the football games and I was like, "Well jeez, there's plenty of room for my letter *(Fighting tears.)* they just didn't do it." And I said to my partner Bill, "We're in this little world where everything's okay like in our neighborhood and in our jobs, but there's all these people around us that are thinkin' this shit." And, I drove out to the prairie and screamed until my throat hurt. It really broke my spirit when they refused to print my letter.

What am I gonna do with this? You know, what AM I gonna do?

JEFFREY LOCKWOOD. Laramie had this moment. There was a moment of self-reflection.

NARRATOR. Jeffrey Lockwood.

JEFFREY LOCKWOOD. But it was just too frightening. The Matthew Shepard murder flies in the face of who we are, the story we've told ourselves and so you've either got to radically adjust your story or you've got to throw out the data. And so far what we've done is throw out the data.

REGGIE FLUTY. Shame is a funny thing. It makes you really look at yourself hard, you know? And when you have that kind of thing happen in your town, and it hurts a whole community, where you think, "Yeah, that can happen here." And it's hard when you're very ashamed of yourself to stand up and say, "Yeah, we screwed up." Instead we start making excuses, and pointing the blame at somebody else or others—we do that as individuals, we do it as a community, we do it as a nation. And that's what I think we've done.

SUSAN SWAPP. But still it would be wrong to think that the whole community believes that it wasn't a hate crime.

NARRATOR. Laramie resident Susan Swapp.

SUSAN SWAPP. That would be an unfair characterization of Laramie. I don't believe that. That's the kind of thing that people say, "Oh, Laramie believes that it was a robbery or drug deal gone bad." That makes me really angry. And it's not true. I don't believe that.

Moment: Potluck

LEIGH FONDAKOWSKI. We spoke to John Dorst, a folklorist at the University of Wyoming. We asked him if he had seen the editorial in the *Boomerang* on the anniversary of Matthew's death.

GREG PIEROTTI. And then we asked him, "So as a folklorist, can you tell us how this change in the story occurred here in Laramie?"

JOHN DORST. As a folklorist, I can tell you that there's a desire for communities to own and control their history. And when that gets taken away, a "reaction formation" occurs. You start with more formed things, the facts of the case or the court proceedings. And the folkloric process is one of winnowing and reduction, the paring away of detail until frequently the actual events—something you might call a story—dissipate. And that's what folklorists call the genre of rumor. But can I ask you—what kinds of versions have you heard?

GREG PIEROTTI. Well, Leigh and I were invited to a potluck last night where we talked to several people.

JOHN DORST. And what did they say?

GEORGE. I heard it was a drug deal gone bad. I don't think it was a hate crime. Laramie is not that kind of a community. The Eastern media had an idea of who we are but that's not who we are. It could have happened anywhere.

GREG PIEROTTI. Yes. One of the responses we often get to the play when people see it is "This could be my town. Laramie is just like my town."

GEORGE. That's it. That's right.

GREG PIEROTTI. But does that mean that there is no homophobia in Laramie, or does it mean that there is also homophobia in other towns?

GEORGE. Laramie is not a homophobic community. There might be individuals who are, but we are not a homophobic community.

JOHN DORST. In some ways it's more acceptable to say yes we do have drug problems in a place like Laramie. It's something you can fix. Hatreds and especially homophobic hostilities seem less controllable.

BEN. I still haven't decided either way, but to say this was a hate crime is not taking the context of the situation into consideration.

LEIGH FONDAKOWSKI. What do you mean?

BEN. That these guys were not virtuous. They were in an environment where drugs and promiscuity prevail and nothing good is going to come from a situation like that. Matthew Shepard missed the signs. Those two guys must have been giving off signs that they were not to be trusted, but he missed them.

LEIGH FONDAKOWSKI. How do you know this?

BEN. I've heard from friends, people I know, people I've hung out with who have told me that they were tweaking.

LEIGH FONDAKOWSKI. But the cops determined they were not tweaking, not on drugs.

BEN. Well, the guys I'm talking about, I would believe them over the cops. I don't trust authority figures in general, and I don't trust the Laramie Police.

JOHN DORST. That kind of insider knowledge. That's another

way that people claim control over their stories. You know we're the insiders, we know what really happened.

JIM. Those three guys were a train wreck just waiting to happen. I also heard there was something sexual there too.

GREG PIEROTTI. How do you know? You say these things like you know they are facts, but there was a trial with a lot of evidence given that negated a lot of what you are saying.

JIM. Oh. Well, I hadn't heard that. I guess maybe a little bit of fact and fiction that mixes together and that's how you get an urban myth. It's an urban myth.

JOHN DORST. People will back away very quickly if they're putting forward a rumor type thing and you question it further. When you do push back, you are violating the "convention of rumor." People inevitably back away. The convention is that you DON'T contend it. That's one of the reasons that it can circulate as sort of this vague, "I don't know where I heard this." It's just sort of in the air. It's just around. That's the nature of rumor. So how do you have a certain degree of sympathy for a community that has been traumatized in this way? And at the same time not abandon the ethical and moral position that you would want to take against these rumors? It's a very messy business.

So for me, this is definitely the issue—maybe the core issue here in Laramie—the desire for control over memory or over history.

SUSAN SWAPP. But still it would be wrong to think that the whole community believes that it wasn't a hate crime.

NARRATOR. Laramie resident Susan Swapp.

SUSAN SWAPP. That would be an unfair characterization of Laramie. I don't believe that. That's the kind of thing that people say, "Oh, Laramie believes that it was a robbery or drug deal gone bad." And it's not true. I don't believe that.

BETH LOFFREDA. Of course this story is getting retold.

NARRATOR. Beth Loffreda.

BETH LOFFREDA. Not just here, but nationally. I mean, a congresswoman from North Carolina just claimed that calling Matthew Shepard's murder a hate crime was a "hoax." So I find it enraging, this idea that it's okay to enmesh us in these dishonesties. Where does that stop? It inflicts real damage to the world we live in, when we all agree to lie, so that we don't have to feel sympathy for someone that so many people feel it's more proper to be disgusted by. I just think it's awful.

Moment: Nikki Elder

NIKKI ELDER. When Matthew was killed, my oldest daughter was a preschooler.
NARRATOR. Nikki Elder, Laramie High School teacher.
NIKKI ELDER. Now she's fifteen and she has this wonderful friend, this sweet boy, and recently they were on the bus, and these other boys say to him, "Oh, we should just tie you to a fence on the outskirts of town." These other boys said that to this boy. They're high school kids now so they were what, four or five years old when Matt was killed? My daughter reported them, and I am very proud of her for that, and the principal pulled them right in. This is something that was taken very seriously in Laramie. But ten years later, you see the cycle happening again.

Moment: The Investigating Officers

Acting note: DeBree and O'Malley should not be played as defensive here. They are confident in the facts and should display all the authority of their offices.

ANDY PARIS. After hearing so many rumors about what happened that night we decided to talk to the officers who investigated Matthew's case: Rob DeBree and Dave O'Malley.
We are hearing other people say that McKinney and Henderson didn't target Matthew Shepard because he was gay.
DAVE O' MALLEY. Their own statement was, they went into a bathroom, they hatched the plan to pretend that they were gay, to try to befriend Matt, get him isolated. Okay.
ROB DEBREE. Henderson went into great detail as to how they planned it… They knew he was gay, that one of them would pretend to be gay in hopes of luring him out. You're definitely focusing on an individual because you assume he is gay.

37

ANDY PARIS. But we keep hearing this was a robbery gone bad. That Henderson and McKinney only wanted money.

ROB DEBREE. That's the beginning, and granted robbery was a part of it, but it went way beyond that. Matthew would have given his wallet to McKinney a few blocks from the bar. That's right up here on the corner, and that would have been the end of the robbery. It went way beyond the wallet.

DAVE O' MALLEY. McKinney's own statement is, "I only had to hit him one time to get his wallet." But then *why* drive this young man out of the city limits, tie him to a fence and hit him in the head and face nineteen to twenty-one times with the butt end of a great big gun.

ANDY PARIS. How else would you answer these rumors?

ROB DEBREE. A lot of people never got to see the crime scene except for law enforcement. The attack point—it was a true battle. They tie him, they beat him viciously. In fact his watch is located almost thirty feet away from him. You could see the marks of blood spatterings in a wide variety of different areas. About twenty yards. We found blood spatter all over. And Henderson made the statement that Matthew broke free and tried to run. But of course didn't get very far.

ANDY PARIS. But several people have said that McKinney and Henderson were involved with drugs that night.

ROB DEBREE. We've proven that there was no drugs on board with McKinney and Henderson…just NONE. Even through their own statements the last time they did the meth was two to three weeks prior. We had blood samples from both of them that night because they both ended up in the hospital. *(Frustrated.)* That was a proved thing at the trial… Look, I wish people had seen. When McKinney was in a detention facility he had no problem telling everybody he had killed the faggot…he was his own little hero. In fact, the day of his sentencing he was smiling. He had just said, supposedly, that he felt so bad for the family, for what he had done, but he goes over in the detention facility and he's smiling to the other prisoners. So…I don't care what McKinney tries to come up with now, or Henderson. I really don't care. I have been in law enforcement going on my twenty-seventh year… I don't know how many times I've addressed it. I don't know what we need to do to get people to understand.

CATHERINE CONNOLLY. We in Laramie need to understand our history and our place in history.

NARRATOR. Catherine Connolly.

CATHERINE CONNOLLY. It's important for us to do that, and we will do that. We MUST do that.

NARRATOR. Stephen Belber.

STEPHEN BELBER. After meeting with Russell's grandmother, I took her advice and wrote to him asking if I could visit and interview him. I heard nothing for three weeks. But today I received the following letter:

RUSSEL HENDERSON. Dear Mr. Belber, I got your letter and I've considered your proposal to talk with me and I've decided that I will do it.

As you know, I've been reluctant to talk to anyone. But I think if there is something I might say that will help someone else to understand or to maybe help them not make the same mistakes I did, then it will be worth it.

I must admit that I'm not the best with words so I don't know how much I will be able to help but I will tell you that I will be honest with you.

I haven't read or seen the play but maybe once you finish this new part of it you could send me a copy of it.

Respectfully, Russell.

End of Act One

ACT TWO

Moment: Russell Henderson

Acting note: Be careful not to take on a brooding quality when playing Russell. The scene should play briskly.

NARRATOR. Russell Henderson was the first of the two perpetrators to go to trial in Laramie. He was convicted of murder and kidnapping and is serving two consecutive life terms in prison.

STEPHEN BELBER. The folks at the prison's visitor entrance pat me down, lock up my valuables, and stamp my hand. And then I'm ushered though an outdoor corridor, into a vestibule, where doors shut behind me, before another pair opens before me. And then I enter into the visitors' room where I see Russell, sitting at the table with the low partition. He has no attitude, no show. Just a balding, thirty-year-old man in a green jumpsuit.

RUSSEL HENDERSON. Me and Aaron worked together at the roofing company for about three months before that night. We hung out a fair amount. I was working at the Conoco and the roofing place at the same time.

STEPHEN BELBER. Had you ever gotten into drugs?

RUSSEL HENDERSON. Not really. I've never been on like a drug binge.

STEPHEN BELBER. One of the things people keep saying about that night, with Matthew, is that you guys were on the back end of a two-week meth binge.

RUSSEL HENDERSON. *I* wasn't. The last time I'd done any drugs was on my birthday, which was two weeks before that night. And I'd only done a little bit. I don't know about Aaron.

STEPHEN BELBER. And had you ever robbed people before?

RUSSEL HENDERSON. Never. I mean, I was one of those guys who was brought up with values, but I actually *believed* them. I *believed* the values, I was raised not to hurt people, and I agreed.

STEPHEN BELBER. So why'd you go along with Aaron that night?

40

RUSSEL HENDERSON. At first I told Aaron I didn't want to. I kept saying no. But he kept wanting to, so finally I just, I went along.

STEPHEN BELBER. Why?

RUSSEL HENDERSON. I guess I'm more of a follower. And he's a leader. So I just went along.

STEPHEN BELBER. Okay, but when you did rob Matthew, why did you take him to the fence? I mean, you had his wallet in the truck, no?

RUSSEL HENDERSON. We were just gonna rob him and leave him out there, so that he'd be stuck out there.

STEPHEN BELBER. Can you tell me what happened when you got out to the fence?

RUSSEL HENDERSON. Aaron told me to tie him to the fence. But I didn't actually tie him. I just wrapped the rope around his hands. Because, you know, I figured... I wanted him to be able to leave.

STEPHEN BELBER. And so, when Aaron started hitting him over and over—?

RUSSEL HENDERSON. I just wanted it to stop. I wanted to hide. Make it go away. So I just did what I always did. I hid. Tried to escape. Pretend like it's not happening. Instead of being more... strong. I didn't think I could stop him. That's why I went back to the truck.

STEPHEN BELBER. Well one story I've always heard is that you tried to stop him from beating Matthew.

RUSSEL HENDERSON. *(A nod.)* Let's just say I tried to stop him but I didn't try enough. You know what I mean? I didn't... It's mostly just, you know, shame. That I didn't do more.

STEPHEN BELBER. What do you wish you'd have done differently?

RUSSEL HENDERSON. I wish I'd have stopped him. I made the wrong choice to go along with it from the beginning; I made the wrong choice to tie him up, I made the wrong choice not to get help. I've thought a lot about it, about every single thing I did; and I just wish I could...change what I did.

STEPHEN BELBER. Your grandmother told me you'd taken a victim empathy course?

RUSSEL HENDERSON. Yeah. And what they have you do is actually draft a letter to your victim. Which I did, and I chose Matthew's family, because even though Matthew was my victim, so was his family. And a part of that is that you write about a time in your life when *you* were a victim.

41

STEPHEN BELBER. What did you write about for when *you* were a victim?

RUSSEL HENDERSON. About when my mom was killed. Which was, obviously, different circumstances, and a different level of attention, but, you know, we both lost family members, in violent crimes...

STEPHEN BELBER. Can you tell me more about how your mom died?

RUSSEL HENDERSON. My mom was killed in Laramie; she was raped, and then the guy just left her on the side of the road. She tried to make it back to town, but she froze to death... Writing about that really...helped me, it made me understand the pain I had caused to Matt and to Matt's parents and family.

STEPHEN BELBER. Is that the letter you tried to send to Judy Shepard?

RUSSEL HENDERSON. It...prepared me for what I wrote her.

STEPHEN BELBER. And did you ever hear back from her?

RUSSEL HENDERSON. I don't even know if she read it.

STEPHEN BELBER. What do you say to people who say you're just saying you're sorry now because you want your sentence reduced?

RUSSEL HENDERSON. I don't know. I can't really do anything about that. For a long time all I thought about and what I was sorry for was the whole world hating me. But now, all I would want to say to you is that I'm sorry for what I did to Matt's family. That's what I would want to say.

I still have trouble about what I did, what I didn't do, and how I'm going to deal with that for the rest of my life. I still wake up; I'm still trying to figure it out, why I did what I did.

STEPHEN BELBER. As you think about your future, do you, you know, do you have hope?

RUSSEL HENDERSON. *Hope?*

STEPHEN BELBER. Yeah.

RUSSEL HENDERSON. For what?

STEPHEN BELBER. I dunno. To get out?

RUSSEL HENDERSON. No. I don't have hope for that. Mostly no. I try to just accept it.

STEPHEN BELBER. Are you at all religious?

RUSSEL HENDERSON. I mean, I grew up as a Mormon, and my grandmother still is. She's really involved with the church, but after this all happened, I got excommunicated. And so I've had trouble sort of dealing with that.

STEPHEN BELBER. So what went wrong, Russell?

RUSSEL HENDERSON. The only explanation I can offer is I was young and I thought I was strong and I could handle whatever the world could throw at me, and when this happened I realized that none of this was true. I was weak and scared and all I did was hide from it. Every day I play out in my mind what I could have done or what I should have done but none of it matters because I didn't do it.

STEPHEN BELBER. How's your relationship with Aaron these days?

RUSSEL HENDERSON. We're cordial. You know, we're sort of attached forever by this thing, so... He has his friends, I have mine, but we see each other every day. We're cordial... I mean, he's a character, you know? He's the one people are gonna want to hear.

Moment: Institutional Change

CATHERINE CONNOLLY. There was certainly the hope and the desire that something like this would never happen again but then you just constantly see the stats of hate crime violence; violence towards gays in this country is going up, not down.

And we still haven't passed any kind of hate crimes legislation in this state.

But one shouldn't be naïve—we certainly know from any kind of social movement that we still have racism, we still have sexism, those haven't gone away.

There's a whole lot more that needs to be done and I'm a person who believes in institutional change so that's why I'm running for a House seat in the Wyoming Legislature.

STEPHEN BELBER. On November fourth, 2008, Catherine Connolly won that House seat, becoming the first openly gay member of the Wyoming Legislature.

43

Moment: Language of Delay

STEPHEN BELBER. Six months later, we traveled back to Laramie to conduct more interviews. The recession finally caught up with Wyoming. The week we were there, the university announced it had to cut eighteen million dollars from its budget at the request of the governor. The front page of the *Boomerang* announced forty-five people lost their jobs at the university.

Days later, funding for domestic partner benefits finally came to a vote.

From a University of Wyoming press release:

NARRATOR. The University of Wyoming has been considering a domestic partnership initiative for several years now. Today, at a special closed-door meeting the Board of Trustees approved funding for domestic partnership benefits.

(Sotto voce.) The approved plan will create a program under which vouchers for health insurance coverage will be offered for domestic partners of either sex of UW employees and is patterned after those at other universities.

ZACKIE SALMON. Woo hoo! Even in the middle of the Wyoming prairie change has occurred!

NARRATOR. Zackie Salmon.

ZACKIE SALMON. It only took ten years! BUT IT PASSED!

BETH LOFFREDA. It's good news.

NARRATOR. Beth Loffreda.

BETH LOFFREDA. The vote was six to five so we feel lucky it came out okay. *But*…there is this language of delay in the plan:

NARRATOR. The board's vote directs that the system be implemented only when UW President Tom Buchanan determines it is fiscally feasible to do so. UW recently announced sweeping budget cuts.

BETH LOFFREDA. That language of delay just makes me crazy. As if nobody's getting hurt or burdened while we just wait a little longer. The spectacular dishonesty of people in power who enjoy all of the benefits, right, that they are denying to other people.

Moment: Defense of Marriage Act (DOMA)

NARRATOR. Leigh Fondakowski.

LEIGH FONDAKOWSKI. We met up again with Cathy Connolly a few months after her term as a representative began to ask her how it was going.

CATHERINE CONNOLLY. Well, I went through freshman training in the House of Representatives, so I'm a freshman. And one of my first orders of business was a defense of marriage bill introduced in the House—a constitutional amendment; it was one of *those*. Like Proposition 8 in California. Our bill was called Resolution 17, a bill defining marriage in Wyoming as being exclusively between a man and woman.

Bills first must be heard and passed out of a committee before they are debated on the House floor. I testified in that committee against the bill. I came out in that committee. I brought in my son's birth certificate. My son's birth certificate has two women on it, recognized by the State of New York. And I said, *(She holds her son's birth certificate.)* "Look, we're recognized as a family unit, and we came here and raised our son and Wyoming didn't fall apart because of it."

But the resolution had enough support to make it out of committee, and therefore it made it to the floor of the House.

CLERK. House Joint Bill Resolution 17: A joint resolution proposing to amend the Wyoming Constitution specifying that a marriage between a man and a woman shall be the only legal union that shall be valid or recognized in the state of Wyoming.

CATHERINE CONNOLLY. The bill was introduced by a Republican, Owen Peterson, so he spoke first:

PETERSON. Mr. Chairman. There are many reasons why the institution of marriage between a man and a woman benefits society. More than thirty years of studies have shown that kids raised by two married biological parents are more successful and better behaved in school, more likely to attend and graduate college, less likely to live in poverty, less likely to drink or do drugs, less likely to commit crimes, less likely to be physically abusive.

Now I can't stand here and say that because there is a marriage between a man and a woman everything is hunky-dory with society, that's not the case. But this research has shown that children that have daily access to the daily complimentary ways that mothers and fathers present, studies have shown that that has a definite significant impact, and since I have three children, seven grandchildren, that is definitely the way.

CATHERINE CONNOLLY. And he went on for probably ten minutes…and in the Wyoming Legislature, we have a desk mate—and my desk mate, she finally leans over to me and says:

DESK MATE. You don't have to hear this. You don't have to.

CATHERINE CONNOLLY. And I just got up and walked out, but one of my colleagues who is incredibly conservative, I walked by him and he said to me:

CONSERVATIVE COLLEAGUE. *(Note: This was said very gently.)* I'm sorry. This will be over soon.

CATHERINE CONNOLLY. So I went back to my seat.

PETERSON. Mr. Chairman, since the beginning of civilization, in every known society, governments have recognized a marriage between a man and a woman because it provides the next generation outstanding citizens and is the only means of melding two sexes into a stronger and more complete whole.

I exert the body to move forward and pass this resolution. I will relinquish the floor and stand for questions.

CATHERINE CONNOLLY. So that happened. We needed twenty-one votes to strike it down. We had only nineteen Democrats and three or four of them didn't want to do it given their districts. So, we're gonna lose. We're gonna lose. Then another conservative, Representative Childers, spoke.

CHILDERS. Ladies and gentlemen, I too have been married forty-six years. I have three lovely children and I'm very proud of them. Two are sons with two granddaughters and another one on the way. My third daughter lives in Montana. *(Pause.)* She's gay. She has a significant other. They aren't married because Montana's law doesn't allow it. But folks to my dying breath there's not anybody in this country could say that she is a terrible person, or a something person that needs to be—have their rights restricted. She lives a quiet life with her significant other. Most people would never know she's gay, and quite frankly until she graduated from college my wife and I didn't know it. Her freshman year, very first semester, we had a counselor say she better come home. And why? Well, we had no idea. But she came home because the counselor was very concerned about what was happening to her. And quite frankly I think there was a possibility of suicide. She has grown from that point to a very stable person, and productive and does things for society quite well. She represents a healthcare faction for the Physical Therapy Association—travels all over the nation. Smart? Oh Lord, she's smart. Good person. But what we're doing with this constitutional amendment, should she have lived here, is to deny her civil rights. You know folks, I grew up in the South. The town that I grew up in was segregated... Now you think about a gay person in redneck country, I can say that 'cause in northeast Texas that's redneck country. And the prejudice against the gay and lesbian community is there I'll guarantee ya. And that hate in their eyes or the fear in the gay person's eyes is there. Do we want a society in this state to do that? Do we want to deny the rights of a gay and lesbian person? I don't think so. Ladies and gentlemen this bill is wrong. And I suggest you vote against it.

CATHERINE CONNOLLY. It was incredibly moving. But at this point we have counts of where we think this was going. So it was gonna pass. We had probably ten or fifteen undecided. And then one last Republican stood up. A very powerful man in Wyoming politics, maybe running for governor in the next election, he got up and he said:

REPUBLICAN MAN. We are the state of Matthew Shepard and the state of *Brokeback Mountain*, but we're also the state of Esther Hobart Morris, first female justice of the peace in the United States, and Nellie Tayloe Ross, first woman to serve as a governor of any U.S. state—and—if we let Resolution 17 out of this body—our state will be ripped apart at the seams quite frankly. It will divide families, divide churches, divide neighbors, divide friends, and will cause a political havoc that this state hasn't seen in decades. I urge you to vote against this bill.

REPRESENTATIVE COHEE. We have heard this issue and I think it is time to cast the vote. Mr. Chairman, I call for the question.

CATHERINE CONNOLLY. And then came the vote.

CLERK. The question having been called, the chief clerk will call the roll. Peterson.

PETERSON. Aye.

CLERK. Barbuto.

BARBUTO. No.

CLERK. Brechtel.
BRECHTEL. Aye.
CLERK. Brown.
BROWN. No.
CLERK. Blake.
BLAKE. No.
CLERK. Buchanan.
BUCHANAN. Aye.
CLERK. Cannady.
CANNADY. Aye.
CLERK. Childers.
CHILDERS. No.
CLERK. Connolly.
CONNOLLY. No.
CLERK. Davidson.
DAVIDSON. Aye. *(Clerk goes sotto voce.)*
CLERK. Edmonds.
EDMONDS. Aye.
CLERK. Hallinan.
HALLINAN. Aye.
CLERK. Harshman.
HARSHMAN. Aye.
CLERK. Harvey.
HARVEY. Aye.
CLERK. Hales.
HALES. No.
CLERK. Hammons.
HAMMONS. No.
CLERK. Lockhart.
LOCKHART. Aye.
CLERK. Madden.
MADDEN. Aye.
CLERK. Peasley.
PEASLEY. Aye.
CLERK. Semlek.
SEMLEK. Aye.
CATHERINE CONNOLLY. So we are the state of Matthew Shepard and the state of *Brokeback Mountain* and as ten years has gone on, people resent it—people resent that they are from the place where "that gay kid was killed." *(Clerk comes back to full volume.)*

CLERK. Seward.
SEWARD. No.
CLERK. Simpson.
SIMPSON. Aye.
CLERK. Stubson.
STUBSON. Aye.
CLERK. Wallis.
WALLIS. No.
CLERK. That concludes the vote. We will review the count.
CATHERINE CONNOLLY. But in the end—Resolution 17, our defense of marriage bill, didn't pass—it failed by thirty-five to twenty-five. It failed. And it was Republicans. It was Republicans that defeated it.

Moment: Measuring Change #2

NARRATOR. Andy Paris.
ANDY PARIS. We had a chance to talk again with Dave O'Malley, chief investigating officer for the Matthew Shepard case for the Laramie Police Department.
DAVE O' MALLEY. You wanna talk about change? You know, quite frankly before all of this happened, that's how I believed, pretty homophobic. The word "faggot" rolled off my tongue more often than "I love you" to my kids. But after what happened to Matt I was thrust into a situation where I had to interact with the gay community. And those kids were fleeing town. And that was where I started realizing what a hate crime was. I mean look, people get killed in liquor store robberies all the time; but I don't think twice about going in and buying a six-pack of beer. But here kids— and adults too—were leaving Laramie, and that fear, that's when I started realizing—I mean that's…that's terroristic. I don't know why it takes a young man like Matt dying for someone like me to start losing my ignorance, but that's what it took.

So, DeBree and I went to Washington seven or eight times with Judy Shepard to advocate for the federal hate crimes bill. But here it is, three administrations later, and the legislation's still not a reality. In 1998 it was called the Hate Crimes Prevention Act. In

2007, it was renamed the Matthew Shepard and James Byrd, Jr. Hate Crimes Prevention Act. And when it reached the floor of the House just this year, you won't believe some of the things we heard. *(On upstage screen, video appears of Congresswoman Virginia Foxx.)*
VIRGINIA FOXX. *(Video.)* The hate crimes bill, that's called the Matthew Shepard bill. It is named after a very unfortunate incident that happened where a young man was killed. But we know that the young man was killed in the commitment of a robbery. It wasn't because he was gay. This bill was named for him. The Hate Crimes bill was named for him. But it—it's really a hoax.
DAVE O' MALLEY. And Judy Shepard was in the gallery that day. And she had to sit there and listen to that.

Moment: Remorse

NARRATOR. Greg Pierotti.
GREG PIEROTTI. Aaron McKinney is in state penitentiary in Virginia. I sent Aaron a letter asking if he would meet with me. I never heard back so I called Father Roger again to see if he could help.
FATHER ROGER. Well, I will send him a letter too. And, Greg, ask Aaron about his remorse. Those of us who have done things in our lives that are really significant in their gravity, we are going to alter our remorse throughout the course of our lives. Sometimes that remorsefulness gets chinked one way, and then it gets bent a different way and then hopefully, by the time we die, we have it in the correct perspective. I think Aaron is not finished finalizing his experience of remorse. And remorse is something we *all* need to think about. So you ask him about that. And, Greg, do him justice.
GREG PIEROTTI. Father, how do I do Aaron McKinney justice?
FATHER ROGER. *(Surprised.)* You get to know him, Greg. Let him teach you what it's like to be Aaron McKinney, okay? Now, I will write him today for you.

Moment: Aaron McKinney

Acting note: Please do not play Aaron as a sinister or brooding character. Aaron is a "regular guy" and the tension between what he says and his matter-of-fact disposition is chilling.

NARRATOR. Aaron never replied to Father Roger's letter. But Greg put in a request to visit with Aaron anyway, and the prison approved it. Greg went ahead and booked a flight. He went through all the paperwork and questions and metal detectors and pat-downs. As Greg headed into the prison, he still didn't know if Aaron was going to see him. But as he passed through the last sally port to the visiting room, there Aaron was, in the very first seat. He had very bright green eyes and a lot of tattoos on his arms. One on his right forearm said: "Trust No One."

AARON MCKINNEY. That's it. You can't reach over the partition again.

GREG PIEROTTI. Oh, okay. Thank you so much for seeing me, Aaron.

AARON MCKINNEY. I threw your letter out, I thought you were the media. And there was no way I was gonna talk to you. I hate the fuckin' media. But when I got the letter from Father Roger that you were friends of him I thought—okay yeah. I'll see you. Father Roger is a good guy, he is definitely family.

GREG PIEROTTI. Yeah, I love Father Roger.

AARON MCKINNEY. Yeah. A big smile and the wind blowing back his face, that's my picture of Father Roger.

GREG PIEROTTI. Those are amazing tattoos you have.

AARON MCKINNEY. Thanks. Yeah. A couple'a guys in here do real good work. Homemade ink, hook a guitar string up to a battery. But it's not allowed, so you gotta have someone watching for the guards and you always gotta stop when they come so it takes forever. I'm working on a full shirt.

GREG PIEROTTI. Wow. That's cool. So, uh, you know we wrote a play and that you are a character in it, right?

AARON MCKINNEY. Yeah, I heard about it. I heard about it,

51

but I never saw it. I don't know what I say in it.

GREG PIEROTTI. Well, it's all your words. We used your actual words from when Rob DeBree interviewed you. That was all we had of yours. What was in the trial transcripts.

AARON MCKINNEY. *(Apparently genuinely surprised.)* The trial transcripts?

GREG PIEROTTI. Because when we were interviewing people we couldn't actually speak to you.

AARON MCKINNEY. Okay.

GREG PIEROTTI. And we are checking back with the characters ten years later. So that's why I am here.

AARON MCKINNEY. Okay.

GREG PIEROTTI. So what's it been like in prison for you all this time?

AARON MCKINNEY. This place isn't too good. It's freezing. *(Pointing to his thin, green jumpsuit.)* This and a real thin blanket is all you get even for outside and in the winter. It's fucking freezing. And they keep us in our cells here all but one hour a day.

GREG PIEROTTI. What do you do for twenty-three hours a day in your cell?

AARON MCKINNEY. Nothin' much. Work out, sleep, watch TV. I don't read much. I read a couple of books. I read *Ice Man*, did you ever read that?

GREG PIEROTTI. No.

AARON MCKINNEY. It's great, man. It's about this hit man for the mob. And then I read a couple of books about the Nazis. They were pretty informative. I'm pretty interested in that.

GREG PIEROTTI. Okay. And what about the other places you have been?

AARON MCKINNEY. Well, they've moved me and Russ like five times. We are always together.

Wyoming was shit. Nevada was kind of scary. A lot of gangs. Got moved to Texas twice. Texas was a dream, man. It was pretty free. I wish I could get put back in Texas.

GREG PIEROTTI. Is there any chance that you will?

AARON MCKINNEY. No telling.

GREG PIEROTTI. And is there any chance as far as your lawyers are concerned that you will get out of prison altogether?

AARON MCKINNEY. Man, I'm never getting outta here. You kiddin'? I am like the poster child for hate-crime murders. Shit, for years, after anything happened to a gay person they thrown my picture up there too. I'm never gettin' out. And you gotta resign yourself to it or you go crazy. So you just try to enjoy yourself. Russ might get out. Shit, he should get out. He doesn't belong in here.

GREG PIEROTTI. Do you see much of him in here?

AARON MCKINNEY. Every day. He is a good friend. I'd give my life for Russ. He didn't do anything. I told him, I would do anything in my power to get him out of here.

GREG PIEROTTI. So he didn't do anything that night?

AARON MCKINNEY. Nothing.

GREG PIEROTTI. Can you talk more about what did happen that night?

AARON MCKINNEY. Well, I have a pretty bad memory of the whole thing.

GREG PIEROTTI. So what do you remember, Aaron?

AARON MCKINNEY. We definitely picked him up to rob him. I was dealing at the time, and I had just got this beautiful gun. Almost brand-new Smith & Wesson .357 Magnum with a ten-inch barrel. Fucking huge beautiful gun. So we went to the Fireside and I was definitely in the mindset to rob.

GREG PIEROTTI. So you were looking for someone to rob?

AARON MCKINNEY. Yeah.

GREG PIEROTTI. So why Matt?

AARON MCKINNEY. Well, he was overly friendly. And he was obviously gay. That played a part in the part of his weakness. His frailty. And he was dressed nice. Looked like he had money. I think he was drinkin' Heineken. Some expensive beer. And it looked like he had a buncha money in his wallet. It only ended up being about thirty dollars. But so, when he asked us for a ride, I said definitely, man. It was gonna be easy.

GREG PIEROTTI. Okay. So it started as a robbery. But you said you picked Matt because he was gay and you've said many times that you don't like gay people.

AARON MCKINNEY. I don't.

GREG PIEROTTI. So it sounds like his being gay did have something to do with it.

AARON MCKINNEY. It's a possibility. The night I did it, I did have hatred for homosexuals. That mighta played a small part.

GREG PIEROTTI. So you're telling me hatred toward gays played a part.

AARON MCKINNEY. It might have played a small part, yeah.

GREG PIEROTTI. In your initial interview with Rob DeBree, you said he slid his hand like he was going to grab your balls and that was why you started hitting him.

AARON MCKINNEY. I said that?

GREG PIEROTTI. In your interview.

AARON MCKINNEY. Then it might have happened. I barely remember that interview at all. That's what I said?

GREG PIEROTTI. That's definitely what you said.

AARON MCKINNEY. Maybe that happened. Like I said, I barely remember anything.

GREG PIEROTTI. What do you remember? You got him in the truck…

AARON MCKINNEY. Yeah, so we got him in the truck and we're drivin'. I had the gun back behind the seat. And I reached back, grabbed it, stuck it in his face, you know, like "rob time." I even poked him in the eye with it. You want to be aggressive when you're robbin' folks, so they believe you'll follow through.

GREG PIEROTTI. *(Somewhat speechless.)* So…you made him give you his wallet.

AARON MCKINNEY. Yeah, I made him give me his wallet. I do remember one thing that was eerie. He didn't seem scared at all. He was just looking at me. Even when I was hitting him in the truck, *(He bangs his fist into the center of his forehead.)* he just kept staring at me.

GREG PIEROTTI. But you were doing some pretty scary things, Aaron. You stuck a huge .357 Magnum in his face. You poked him in the eye with it, hit him in the head with it. Couldn't he have just been in shock?

AARON MCKINNEY. I never thought'a that. Yeah maybe. He was complying with my demands. But even when I tied him up to the fence, it was odd too. He really didn't seem to be scared.

GREG PIEROTTI. So what happened next?

AARON MCKINNEY. I took the gun by the barrel, so I was holding it like a bat. And I just beat him in the head with it.

GREG PIEROTTI. Okay.

AARON MCKINNEY. Yeah. Then he made a real weird noise and slumped over—you know like they say people make a noise when they give up the ghost.

GREG PIEROTTI. But he didn't give up the ghost. He held on for six more days.

AARON MCKINNEY. Yeah.

GREG PIEROTTI. Okay. So I just want to go back a minute. You said you tied him up?

AARON MCKINNEY. Yeah, to the fence.

GREG PIEROTTI. Okay, in Russ's statement he said that he tied Matt to the fence.

AARON MCKINNEY. Yeah?

GREG PIEROTTI. Yeah.

AARON MCKINNEY. *(Pause.)* Well, I don't know. If Russell says he did something then he did it. Russ is a man of his word. But I know I tied him.

GREG PIEROTTI. And so what about the hate crime issue?

AARON MCKINNEY. I don't like gay people, it's true. But as long as they stay outta my way, I got no problem with them. I mean there's guys in here that do that. Nobody really jumps you 'cause you're gay. Unless you're a sex predator. They're like the lowest rung. They get problems here from everyone.

GREG PIEROTTI. Okay. So, let me ask you, in Russell's statement when he pled guilty he told the court he was sorry and felt he deserved to pay the price for what he did. But in your trial you never made much of a statement and so I'm wondering—

AARON MCKINNEY. Do I have remorse?

GREG PIEROTTI. Yes, yeah.

AARON MCKINNEY. You mean do I have remorse? Yeah I got remorse. My dad taught me I should stand tall and be a man. I got remorse that I didn't live the way my dad taught me to live. That I wasn't the man my dad wanted me to be. As far as Matt is concerned, I don't have any remorse. I heard that Matt was a sex predator, and that he preyed on younger guys and had sex with 'em. So when I heard that I was relieved. People might say I am just trying to justify myself, maybe so. As far as I'm concerned, doin' what he was doin', Matt Shepard needed killin'.

GREG PIEROTTI. *(Pause.)* Okay. You know those rumors about Matthew Shepard are not true, Aaron.

AARON MCKINNEY. That's not what I heard.

GREG PIEROTTI. *(Pause.)* Okay. So, you have no remorse at all.

AARON MCKINNEY. Actually, I do feel bad for Matt's dad. That must be hard to lose your son.

GREG PIEROTTI. And what about his mom?

AARON MCKINNEY. For her too, yeah. I feel bad. Still she never shuts up about it, and it's been like ten years, man.

GREG PIEROTTI. Well, Aaron, you brutally murdered her son.

AARON MCKINNEY. *(Conceding.)* Yeah, I know.

GREG PIEROTTI. *(Pause.)* And what about yourself. You have no regret. There is nothing you would change in any way?

AARON MCKINNEY. Hell yeah. All sorts of ways. I was a fucker as a kid. A real fucker. Lied to my dad a lot. I hate that. *(Getting glassy-eyed.)* I fuckin' hate that. He is the greatest dad ever. All the trouble, the drugs. If I could change it I would. I'd go to high school. Graduate.

GREG PIEROTTI. And what if Father Roger were here with us. Could you look him in the eye and honestly tell him you don't feel remorse for Matt?

AARON MCKINNEY. I'd have to. I would never wanna have to do that. You know how I feel about Father Roger. But I couldn't look him in the eye and not…I'd have to tell the truth. I do have remorse, but like I said, for all the wrong reasons. For my dad. For ending up in here. For getting Russ stuck in here. *(Beat.)* If I could go back and not be the one who killed him I would… But I am better off in here, myself. I met guys in here with a real sense of honor. Out there, people'll stab you in the back for a nickel bag. Besides, I am a criminal. I should be around criminals. I always was drawn that way. Shit, I remember crawling through people's doggie doors when I was eight years old to steal their shit. I don't know why, but I was always like this. Nature trumps nurture.

GREG PIEROTTI. Did you see your son ever, since the murder?

AARON MCKINNEY. Never seen him since I was locked up.

GREG PIEROTTI. *(Pause.)* Um okay. Well, I think we're running out of time, Aaron. Before I leave you, I know you say you're never gonna get out of here. But if you did get out, if you were going to get out, where would you go?

AARON MCKINNEY. Shit, I don't know. Italy, maybe or Germany. I am really interested in Germany. But I got some tattoos, some swastikas, and I got "NAZI" across my lower back, in big Old English lettering—looks amazing. I heard they'll put you in jail for that now in Germany. Italy's beautiful though—I would definitely like to see Italy and New York too. I like skyscrapers and you all got the most. That's where you're from right? You guys are lucky. I wish I could go to New York and look at the skyline from the water.

GREG PIEROTTI. Yeah, I really love New York. It's pretty great there.

AARON MCKINNEY. So you getting any pussy while you're down here in Virginia?

GREG PIEROTTI. Aaron, you should know I'm gay. I thought you realized that.

AARON MCKINNEY. Yeah, I thought maybe you were when I first saw you, but I didn't want to say anything 'cause I didn't want to offend you.

GREG PIEROTTI. That doesn't offend me.

AARON MCKINNEY. Okay. Cool.

GREG PIEROTTI. Well Aaron, thank you so much for seeing me.

AARON MCKINNEY. Sure, man, like I said, any friend of Father Roger's. Take it easy.

GREG PIEROTTI. You too. Take it easy.

Moment: Judy Shepard

MOISÉS KAUFMAN. Ten years ago during the trials of the two perpetrators, we met Dennis and Judy Shepard in Laramie. We saw them day after day in the courtroom as they watched the proceedings, and then faced the endless press conferences and media coverage. I sat down with Judy on July eleventh 2009 for our very first formal interview.

(To Judy.) Judy, when I met you at the trials you were a very private person. You didn't want to talk publicly. But now you're a very public figure. You've been lecturing around the country and advocating legislative changes and you've met with Clinton and Obama. How did that happen?

JUDY SHEPARD. I'm just doing…what a mother does when you hurt her children.

After Matt was killed, and we started speaking in public, all I could see in people's eyes was fear, and especially among the young people, that they understood that what happened to Matt could just as easily happen to them, no matter where they lived.

People were saying to me: Do something. You have to do something. I don't think I've done anything spectacular. I've told a story, I've kept Matt's story alive.

MOISÉS KAUFMAN. (Pause.) What can you tell me about him?

JUDY SHEPARD. Well, I think I was pretty sure Matt was gay when he was eight years old. Sometimes, you know, something in the back of your mind. When he dressed up as Dolly Parton for Halloween—for the *third* time. He really worked at it too; he got better each time he did it. He always was very serious about acting. He played the little brother in *Our Town*. When he turned eighteen, he called me in the middle of the night and he said, "Mom, I've got something I've got to tell you." My first reaction was, "What took you so long to tell me?" And he said, "How did you know?" I said, "It's a mom thing."

MOISÉS KAUFMAN. Judy, you know we met with McKinney this time?

JUDY SHEPARD. Yes, I know. It will be interesting to hear what he has to say now. *(Pause.)* When Dennis and I made the recommendation to the judge to take the death penalty off the table for Aaron McKinney...we did that because we just didn't think taking away another son was going to fix anything. And we didn't think Matt would want that either. But it wasn't entirely altruistic. We also understood that if we took the death penalty off the table, we would never have to deal with McKinney again. No appeals, no nothing—he's just gone. And we didn't want Matt's brother Logan to have to deal with that in his life. He would just be gone. So, when McKinney showed up on *20/20* I thought, this is exactly what we didn't want. Here he is again, saying whatever he wants whether it's the truth or not. Changing his story.

MOISÉS KAUFMAN. The changing of the story seems to have really taken hold in Laramie.

JUDY SHEPARD. Yes. I hear the—hate in people's voice—"They robbed him. How could you say it was a hate crime?" I hear people quote the *20/20* story to me still! So...I'm not surprised. I've learned so much about people—what they choose to believe if it makes them feel better. How they have to interpret things to make their own being better, to fit their own image of themselves.

It's not just in Laramie, Moisés, it's nationally too.

MOISÉS KAUFMAN. Yes.

JUDY SHEPARD. Dennis and I were in the gallery when the hate crimes legislation bill was being debated in the U.S. House of Representatives. When Virginia Foxx called Matt's death "a hoax." But honestly, I was expecting it. It was the same rhetoric that we always heard from the opposition, that it wasn't a hate crime; it was the same "changing the story" resurfacing, yet again.

MOISÉS KAUFMAN. Judy, I so vividly remember being at the trial and seeing you then. And now I see this woman and they don't seem like the same person.

JUDY SHEPARD. Yeah. I'm angrier now than I was then. Because it's still happening. *(Begins to cry softly, but does not give in to the tears.)* Sorry.

So here I am at the ten-year mark still fighting. I had to adapt so I could keep doing this. Or, the feeling would be that it would have all happened in vain! I wasn't going to let that happen. Plus, doing the work was my survival! It was how I coped with losing Matt. I could keep him with me all the time. And I was talking to someone and they said, "Well don't you think maybe it's time to let go, don't you think you're keeping Matt alive by doing that?" And I said, "Of course I'm keeping him alive by doing this! That's the point!" That is exactly the point. And I can keep telling the same wonderful stories and my friends don't say, "Judy, you told me that story yesterday and the day before that and the day before that." I can just keep telling it.

NARRATOR. On October twenty-eighth, 2009, just a few months after that interview, Judy stood next to President Barack Obama as he signed the Matthew Shepard and James Byrd, Jr. Hate Crimes Prevention Act into law.

Moment: Legacy

ANDY PARIS. We heard that when the owner took down the fence where Matthew Shepard was found, the pieces were incorporated into other fences. So no one knows where the pieces of the original fence are. This is Jonas Slonaker.

JONAS SLONAKER. I remembered where the place was and I would still go back, and it's...yeah. The fence is gone. Ten years later and the fence is gone... And ten years of snow and rain have washed through there. I mean it's just a place, in the end I guess. And I decided not to go anymore. I had to let it go.

ANDY PARIS. Dave O'Malley.

DAVE O'MALLEY. *(Holding a photograph.)* This is a photograph of the fence that my son took, and some people had been out and kind of made a little memorial there and…I don't know how many people came to town when I was still working at the police department to visit the fence. But I remember one older man—spent thirty years in the military—had to be in the closet through the whole thing. And Matt's death had a huge impact on him. He was from Vermont and one day he just showed up, and I took him out to the fence. I did that with several people, it was important for them. It was important enough for them to come all the way to Laramie to see it! You know? But other than crime scene photographs, this is the only photograph of the fence that I've got.

NARRATOR. We spend the last day of the trip packing our belongings. We're leaving Laramie for the last time. And I find myself thinking about how this story will be told. And about the people we've met. And I think about Matthew.

This is Romaine Patterson. *(All the other actors leave the stage. Romaine sits in the last chair remaining on the set.)*

ROMAINE PATTERSON. At the ten-year anniversary this year they were holding a vigil near my house. And I really wanted to go, but I didn't want to speak. I just wanted to go and be a stranger in the crowd… It's ten years later…and I've just…it's just really recently that I've started to grieve Matt as a person. There was no time for that in those first years. There wasn't an opportunity to sit down and feel the weight of the loss.

I guess over the years…I've kind of defined Matthew in two ways. There's Matt who I knew and the good friend that I had, and then there's Matthew Shepard. And Matthew Shepard is very different from Matt. Matthew Shepard is this iconic hate crime that has happened in our history, and Matthew Shepard is not necessarily about Matt, it's about a community's reaction, it is about the media that followed, it is about the crime, but it's not about Matt. And that was a distinction that I had to make, making my way through this storm over the years, so that I could hold on to who Matt was to me personally, but also to recognize the importance of Matthew Shepard, and that story, and how it was told and will continue to be told throughout the years. *(Romaine gets up and leaves the stage. A light on the empty chair. Blackout.)*

End of Play

The Laramie Project Insights:
Workshops and Resources to Support Your Production

For schools, universities, and theaters producing *The Laramie Project* and/or *The Laramie Project: Ten Years Later*, Tectonic Theater Project wants to nurture the essential community dialogue that the plays have inspired since their premieres. For this purpose, the Company has developed a program entitled The Laramie Project Insights.

The Laramie Project Insights offers three ways to support and engage productions:

1) Laramieproject.org—An online community with resources for people producing, participating in, or interested in *The Laramie Project Cycle*. This site offers members a place to blog, post media, review resource guides for teachers and students, and research information from previous productions. Please visit and join this growing community!

2) Moment Work Training Labs—The Tectonic Company members who created *The Laramie Project Cycle* are available to train your cast in Moment Work, the technique used to build the original production and all of Tectonic's plays.

Moment Work encourages participants to actively engage with the elements of the stage—exploring lights, sound, costumes, movement, character, text, and architecture—to discover their full theatrical potential and inherent poetry. The technique enfranchises artists to collaborate in creating compelling and theatrical storytelling that utilizes all elements of the stage, to stretch their creative capacity while building a layered narrative in their work.

3) Community Workshops/Resources—In addition to anti-bullying and equality, *The Laramie Project Cycle* touches on many issues beyond the stage, and Tectonic wants to help you develop the resources and programming that will best speak to the needs of your production, audiences, and community members.

Tectonic Theater Project also offers the following services:

—Lectures and discussions delivered by Moisés Kaufman and Tectonic Company members

— *The Laramie Project* film viewing and discussion

—Live or virtual Q & A sessions with Tectonic Company members

—Other events and programs to benefit your school, group, or production!

You can also engage with Tectonic through Facebook, Twitter, YouTube, Vimeo, and Flickr.

Interested in learning more? Contact us at:
education@tectonictheaterproject.org, or
212-579-6111

PROPERTY LIST
(Use this space to create props lists for your production)

SOUND EFFECTS
(Use this space to create props lists for your production)